Do Hippos Brush Their Teeth?

How Animals Care for Their Bodies

For Ora and Asa, with love — E.K.
To my parents, for teaching me to find humor in any situation and to follow what makes me happy — J.P.

Text © 2024 Etta Kaner | Illustrations © 2024 Jenna Piechota

Owlkids Books acknowledges the financial support of the Canada Council for the Arts, the Ontario Arts Council, the Government of Canada through the Canada Book Fund (CBF) and the Government of Ontario through the Ontario Creates Book Initiative for our publishing activities.

Owlkids Books gratefully acknowledges that our office in Toronto is located on the traditional territory of many nations, including the Mississaugas of the Credit, the Chippewa, the Wendat, the Anishinaabeg, and the Haudenosaunee Peoples.

Published in Canada by Owlkids Books Inc., 1 Eglinton Avenue East, Toronto, ON M4P 3A1
Published in the US by Owlkids Books Inc., 1700 Fourth Street, Berkeley, CA 94710

Library of Congress Control Number: 2023939171

Library and Archives Canada Cataloguing in Publication

Title: Do hippos brush their teeth? : how animals care for their bodies / written by Etta Kaner ; illustrated by Jenna Piechota.
Names: Kaner, Etta, author. | Piechota, Jenna, illustrator.
Description: Series statement: Do animals? ; 4
Identifiers: Canadiana 20230461484 | ISBN 9781771474931 (hardcover)
Subjects: LCSH: Health behavior in animals—Juvenile literature. | LCGFT: Instructional and educational works.
Classification: LCC QL756.6 .K36 2024 | DDC j591.5—dc23

Edited by Stacey Roderick and Ella Russell | Designed by Danielle Arbour

The display typeface in this book is Manhattan Hand, courtesy of Noble People

MIX
Paper | Supporting responsible forestry
FSC® C104723

Manufactured in Guangdong Province, Dongguan City, China, August 2023, by Toppan Leefung Packaging & Printing (Dongguan) Co., Ltd. Job #BAYDC124

hc   A   B   C   D   E

ONTARIO ARTS COUNCIL
CONSEIL DES ARTS DE L'ONTARIO
an Ontario government agency
un organisme du gouvernement de l'Ontario

Canada Council for the Arts   Conseil des Arts du Canada

Canadä

Publisher of Chirp, Chickadee and OWL
www.owlkidsbooks.com

Owlkids Books is a division of   bayard canada

Do Hippos Brush Their Teeth?

How Animals Care for Their Bodies

Written by **Etta Kaner**

Illustrated by **Jenna Piechota**

Owlkids Books

To stay healthy and care for their bodies, do animals get regular checkups?

So how do animals look after their bodies? Let's find out …

Do hippos brush their teeth?

They have fish friends who clean their teeth instead. After a night of feeding mostly on grass, a hippo heads down to the river. It opens its mouth wide and lets a team of carp fish get to work. The carp use their large mouths to scrape food bits and parasites off the hippo's teeth and mouth. Clean teeth for the hippo, and a free meal for the fish!

Do whales get a good night's sleep?

Instead of a full night's snooze, sperm whales take about eight short power naps each day. Each nap lasts just ten to fifteen minutes. And these school bus–sized whales don't bother lying down to sleep. They float upright in a small group near the surface of the water!

Do frogs drink plenty of water?

YES! (SORT OF)

When they do drink water, Australian water-holding frogs drink a LOT—about half their body weight. But these frogs only do that every two or more years. That's because it rarely rains where they live. So they load up on water when they can and then burrow deep into the earth to wait for the next rain.

Do lizards exercise?

Male lava lizards do push-ups—not to get stronger and bigger but to *look* stronger and bigger. The workout is a way of saying "keep out of my territory" to other males. But if an intruder doesn't leave, the lizards might have a push-up contest. Both males pump up and down, over and over, until one of them finally gives up.

Do pheasants take baths?

YES!

Ring-necked pheasants take *dust* baths. To start, they loosen dry dirt with their feet and rub their chests in it. Then they shake their wings to cover their feathers with dust. The dust helps get rid of oil that makes feathers stick together and parasites that can make birds sick.

Do lions comb their hair?

Like all cats, lions comb their fur using their tongues. Their prickly tongues are covered with hundreds of tiny curved spines made of keratin, the same material as your nails. As lions lick their fur, the spines remove tangles, loose fur, insects, and dirt. Looking gr-r-r-eat!

Do badgers wash their paws after using the toilet?

NO!

But badgers do scoop before they poop. Using their long, sharp claws, badgers dig shallow holes near the edges of the territory where they live. Whenever a badger in the clan (a group that lives together) needs to poop, it heads for one of these "toilet" holes. These toilets also act as "Stay Away" signs to badgers that don't belong to the clan.

Do axolotls use first aid kits?

NO!

Axolotls don't need to. When these Mexican salamanders get cuts, they heal cleanly in a couple of weeks—no bandages needed. It's no problem even if a predator bites off a leg or tail. Axolotls simply regrow them! Regrowing parts of the brain, spinal cord, or heart are a no-brainer, too. And it can happen time and time again. If only humans could do that!

Do giraffes use tissues to wipe their noses?

Giraffes use their long tongues instead. Their tongues
are about twice the length of this book! *And* they are very
flexible. As well as cleaning out their nostrils, giraffes use
their tongues to clean their eyes and ears. What's more,
a thick, sticky saliva (spit) protects the tongue and helps
it heal quickly if it gets cut.

Do caterpillars take medicine?

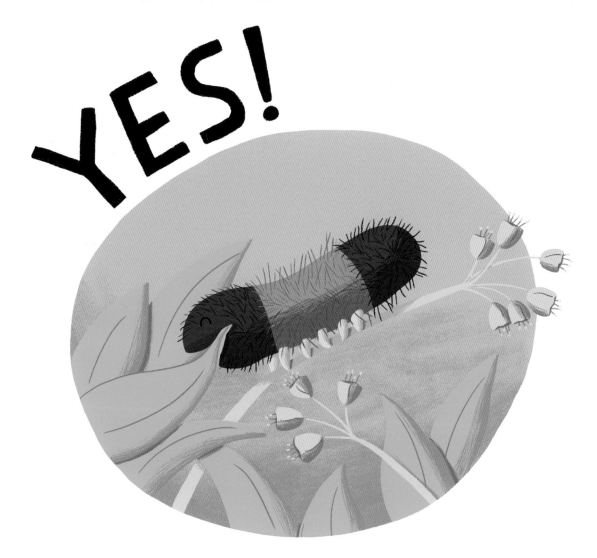

Woolly bear caterpillars eat special plants to cure themselves of a pesky problem. Some types of wasps and flies lay their eggs inside the caterpillar's body. After the eggs hatch, the larvae (young insects) feed on the caterpillar's insides. Eww. But when this happens, the caterpillar can change its diet. It eats plants that are poisonous to the larvae or that will make the caterpillar's body strong enough to resist them.

Do birds use insect repellent?

YES!

Darwin's finches can get very sick from blood-sucking mosquitoes and fly larvae. So the birds pick guava tree leaves and rub them on their feathers. The leaves have a poison that keeps away biting mosquitoes and larvae but doesn't harm the finches. Ahh, that feels better!

Do tortoises take vitamins?

NO!

But gopher tortoises do eat a mineral called calcium to keep their shells and bones strong. They get some calcium from the grasses, wildflowers, and cactuses they feed on. But to get extra calcium, tortoises munch on rocks, feathers, hair, eggshells, animal poop, and even the bones of dead animals!

Do chimpanzees use hand wipes?

YES!
(SORT OF)

Chimpanzees are super picky about staying clean. Luckily, the trees that grow where they live provide plenty of leaf "wipes" for them to pick. Using the fresh leaves to remove mud, sticky fruit juices, blood, poop, and pee makes cleaning their bodies a snap. Family members often clean each other with leaves, too.

All of the animals in this book have special ways of caring for their bodies.

How do *you* look after your body?